Ignite the Dynamite

©Daniel Hagen 2023

First published 2023

Published by Daniel Hagen Ministries

www.danielhagenministries.com

All rights reserved. Without limiting the rights under copyright reserved above, no part of this publication may be reproduced, stored in or introduced into a database and retrieval system or transmitted in any form or any means (electronic, mechanical, photocopying, recording or otherwise) without the prior written permission of both the owner of the copyright and the above publishers. The only exception is brief quotations in printed reviews.

Printed by IngramSpark
SBN: 978-0-6454722-2-6
ISBN Ebook:978-0-6454722-3-3

Unless otherwise specified, all scripture taken from the New King James Version®, Copyright©
1982 by Thomas Nelson. Used by permission. All rights reserved.

Original Cover design by Kathrine Munro (adapted by Beverly Bekker for Ignite the Dynamite Study Guide)

CONTENTS

LESSON 1
Character Before Anointing

LESSON 2
Signs and Wonders with the Truth: Preaching the Full Gospel

LESSON 3
Raising the Dead: Igniting the Power of Resurrection

LESSON 4
Dreams and Visions

LESSON 5
The Power of the Gospel

LESSON 6
Discipled in Healing

LESSON 7
It's for All Believers

LESSON 8
Cessationism

LESSON 9
Ignite the Dynamite! The Empowerment of the Holy Spirit

STUDY NOTES
ADDITIONAL RESOURCES

Lesson 1

Character Before Anointing

Introduction

In this lesson, we will explore the importance of character and Godly living in conjunction with the pursuit of miracle-working power.

While power and anointing are essential, they should be accessed through a relational connection with God.

Our goal is to understand what it means to move in power with the right motives and live a life of holiness.

We will delve into the significance of compassion in action, the role of character in ministry, the trap of deception, the balance of biblical grace versus hyper-grace, and the distinction between weakness and wickedness.

Lesson Outline

3

1. *Compassion In Action* (Matthew 14:14, John 5:19)
- Jesus' intimate relationship with the Father and His compassion for people.
- The importance of spending time with God to align our hearts with His.
- Loving God and loving people as the foundation of ministry.

2. *The Importance of Godly Character* (Matthew 26:41, 1 Peter 1:16)
- Jesus as our example of the need for a strong relationship with the Father.
- The dangers of selfish ambition and wrong motives in ministry.
- The significance of abiding in prayer to avoid temptation and deceitfulness of sin.

3. *The Deceitfulness of Habitual Sin* (Matthew 7:21-23, 1 Timothy 4:1)
- The potential for believers to turn away from righteousness and fall into habitual sin.
- Examples of ministers who fell into sinful practices while still operating in the supernatural.
- The importance of repentance, correction, and developing good character.

4. *The Trap of Deception* (Proverbs 9:10, 1 John 2:1)
- The dangers of fabricating supernatural manifestations for personal gain.
- The impact of counterfeit practices on the genuine move of the Holy Spirit.
- Identity rooted in God's approval rather than gifting.

5. *Biblical Grace vs. Hyper-Grace* (Romans 11:29, Hebrews 8:12)
- Understanding the balance between God's grace and the need for repentance.
- The consequences of turning away from righteousness and practicing iniquity.
- The gifts and calling of God are irrevocable but Godly character is dependent on a repentant heart.

Lesson Outline

6. The Gifts are Irrevocable (Romans 6:6, 2 Corinthians 5:21)
   - The possibility of operating in gifts and calling while still being involved in habitual sin.
   - The warning against falling into wickedness while performing signs and wonders.
   - Differentiating between weakness and wickedness.

7. You Will Know Them by Their Fruit (Matthew 7:20, Galatians 5:22-23)
   - Recognising genuine Christians through the fruit of the Spirit.
   - The importance of character as a witness and reflection of our relationship with God.
   - Balancing grace and holiness without falling into condemnation or complacency.

8. *Weak vs Wicked* (1 Corinthians 10:12, Romans 8:1)
   - Understanding the distinction between moments of weakness and practicing wickedness.
   - Overcoming condemnation and relying on God's forgiveness and cleansing.
   - Embracing our identity in Christ and walking in the Spirit.

Conclusion

- As revival school students, we must prioritise character and Godly living alongside the pursuit of power and anointing.
- True compassion for others flows from an intimate relationship with God.
- We must be aware of the dangers of deceit, habitual sin, and counterfeit practices.
- Through a balanced understanding of biblical grace, repentance, and the gifts of the Spirit, we can live a life marked by holiness and ignite the dynamite of God's power with the right motives.

Reflection

A summary of what you learnt in this lesson:

Reflection

How does this challenge you personally?

_____
_____
_____
_____
_____
_____
_____
_____
_____
_____
_____
_____
_____
_____
_____
_____
_____
_____
_____
_____

Reflection

What is God saying to you personally?

_____
_____
_____
_____
_____
_____
_____
_____
_____
_____
_____
_____
_____
_____
_____
_____
_____
_____
_____

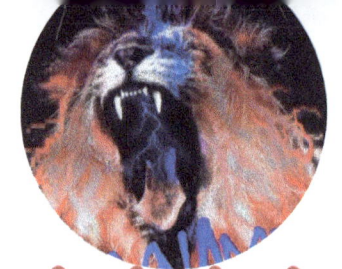

Reflection

Group discussion notes:

APPLICATION

-
-
-
-

APPLICATION

11

AT HOME

How will you apply this practically in your life? (your response to the last reflection question)

- _____
_____
_____
- _____
_____
_____
- _____
_____
_____
- _____
_____
_____
- _____
_____
_____

Lesson 2

Signs & Wonders With The Truth: Preaching the Full Gospel

Introduction

As we pursue the manifestation of God's power, it is essential to remember that our primary goal is to see people saved through the preaching of the gospel.

Signs and wonders serve as a means to lead people to Jesus, and they should be accompanied by the proclamation of the full counsel of God.

In this lesson we will explore the importance of sharing the truth, the necessity of preaching repentance, the balance between grace and truth, the cost of discipleship, and the challenges of addressing hard truths in today's culture.

Lesson Outline

1. *Sharing the Full Counsel of God (1 Corinthians 3:6, Romans 1:16)*
- Understanding the role of signs and wonders in leading people to salvation.
- Recognising the power of the gospel to bring transformation and eternal life.
- Avoiding the neglect of sharing the life-giving message while demonstrating God's power.

2. *The Necessity of Truth and Repentance (John 5:14, John 8:32)*
- Jesus' example of addressing sin and calling for repentance alongside healing.
- Emphasising the importance of turning away from darkness and embracing God's truth.
- Proclaiming the full gospel, including the call to repentance, for genuine transformation.

3. *Balancing Grace and Truth (John 1:14, Romans 6:1-2)*
- Understanding the dual nature of Jesus as full of grace and truth.
- Avoiding the pitfall of focusing solely on grace or truth in our preaching.
- Extending God's grace while upholding the standards of biblical truth.

4. *Signs and Wonders as Signposts (John 6:2, John 14:6)*
- Recognising that signs and wonders attract crowds but are not the ultimate goal.
- Aligning signs and wonders to point people to Jesus, who is the way, the truth, and the life.
- Emphasising the need for discipleship and receiving the truth of God's Word.

Lesson Outline

5. *Truth at the Cost of Followers (John 6:66, John 15:18)*
- Acknowledging that preaching the hard truth may lead to the loss of followers.
- Overcoming the fear of man and prioritising God's truth over man's approval.
- Understanding that persecution and rejection are part of following Jesus.

6. *Today's Hard Truth (John 8:32, Hebrews 4:12)*
- Addressing sensitive topics, such as homosexuality and sexual purity, with grace and love.
- Being willing to confront sin and call for repentance in accordance with God's Word.
- Recognising that the full counsel of God includes the repentance side of the Gospel.

Conclusion

- In our pursuit of signs and wonders, let us never forget the crucial role of truth in leading people to salvation.
- The power of God displayed through miracles should always support and accompany the proclamation of the full gospel.
- While there may be a cost to preaching the truth and addressing hard topics, we must remain committed to following Jesus' example. Let us ignite the dynamite of God's power, operating in signs and wonders, while firmly standing on the foundation of His truth.
- May our ministry be marked by grace and truth, pointing people to Jesus, the only way to eternal life.

Reflection

A summary of what you learnt in this lesson:

Reflection

How does this challenge you personally?

_____
_____
_____
_____
_____
_____
_____
_____
_____
_____
_____
_____
_____
_____
_____
_____
_____

Reflection

What is God saying to you personally?

Reflection

Group discussion notes:

_____
_____
_____
_____
_____
_____
_____
_____
_____
_____
_____
_____
_____
_____
_____
_____
_____
_____
_____
_____
_____

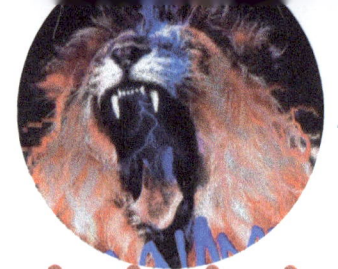

APPLICATION

-
-
-
-
-

APPLICATION

AT HOME

How will you apply this practically in your life? (your response to the last reflection question)

- _____
_____
_____

- _____
_____
_____

- _____
_____
_____

- _____
_____
_____

- _____
_____
_____
_____

Lesson 3

Raising The Dead: Igniting the Power of Resurrection

Introduction

Raising the dead is a subject of profound significance within the Christian faith.
While it may appear less emphasised in our modern culture, its importance cannot be overstated.
In this lesson, we will explore the scriptural foundations of raising the dead, its central role in our belief system, and how it can be applied practically in our lives.
Through the power of God's Word, we will gain a deeper understanding of this miraculous act and its potential for revival in our time.

Lesson Outline

1. Raising the Dead: A Core Belief
- Raising the dead holds a central position in our Christian belief system.
- The resurrection of Jesus Christ is the foundation of our faith, as it ensures the defeat of sin and death. The apostle Paul affirms this in 1 Corinthians 15:17, stating, "And if Christ has not been raised, your faith is futile; you are still in your sins." Thus, raising the dead is not a peripheral topic but an integral part of the Gospel message.

2. Raising the Dead in Scripture
- The Bible provides us with numerous accounts of individuals being raised from the dead, demonstrating God's power over life and death. In the Old Testament, we read about Elijah raising the widow's son (1 Kings 17:17-24) and Elisha raising the Shunammite's son (2 Kings 4:32-37). In the New Testament, Jesus Himself raised the widow's son in Nain (Luke 7:11-17), Jairus' daughter (Luke 8:49-56), and Lazarus of Bethany (John 11:38-44). Additionally, we see Peter raising Tabitha (Acts 9:36-42).
- These examples showcase the continuity of raising the dead throughout the biblical narrative.

3. The Unparalleled Miracle: Raising the Dead
- Raising the dead is a miraculous act that only God can accomplish.
- It stands apart from other signs and wonders, as it defies the power of the enemy.
- The devil can counterfeit certain miracles, but he cannot bestow life or resurrect the dead.
- In Acts 26:8 the apostle Paul speaks of "the hope of the promise made by God to our fathers" referring to the resurrection of the dead. This hope is grounded in God's unrivaled power and ability to restore life.

Lesson Outline

4. How Should We Pray?

- When approaching the task of raising the dead, our prayers should be characterized by both dependence on God and the exercising of our authority in Christ.
- We are encouraged to bring our petitions before God, seeking His guidance, wisdom, and anointing.
- Jesus Himself declared in Matthew 18:18, "Truly I tell you, whatever you bind on earth will be bound in heaven, and whatever you loose on earth will be loosed in heaven." This authority is not to be taken lightly but should be used in alignment with the will of God and His purposes.

5. Living in Faith and Using Our Authority

- Raising the dead requires living a life of unwavering faith and boldly exercising the authority bestowed upon us as believers.
- In Hebrews 11:1, we learn that "faith is the substance of things hoped for, the evidence of things not seen." As we pray and seek God's will, we must firmly believe in His resurrection power and confidently declare His life-giving Word. In Mark 11:23, Jesus teaches us, "Truly I tell you, if anyone says to this mountain, 'Go, throw yourself into the sea,' and does not doubt in their heart but believes that what they say will happen, it will be done for them." This applies to the resurrection power.

6. Modern-Day Testimonies

- The power of raising the dead is not limited to the pages of Scripture; it continues to manifest in the lives of believers today. Countless testimonies bear witness to the ongoing reality of resurrection power. These testimonies serve as tangible reminders that God's power is not confined to a specific era but transcends time and culture. Through the testimonies of individuals like David Hogan, Smith Wigglesworth, and countless others, we are encouraged to press into the supernatural realm and expect God to move mightily in our midst.

Lesson Outline

7. The Call to Ignite the Power of Resurrection
- As believers, we are called to ignite the power of resurrection in our lives and communities. Jesus commissioned His disciples, saying, "And as you go, proclaim, 'The kingdom of heaven is at hand.' Heal the sick, raise the dead, cleanse lepers, cast out demons" (Matthew 10:7-8). This command extends to all believers, as Jesus Himself declared that those who believe in Him would do the works He did and even greater works (John 14:12). Raising the dead is not reserved for a select few; it is an invitation for every believer to step into the fullness of their identity and authority in Christ.

8. Expectancy for Revival
- To ignite the power of resurrection, we must cultivate a spirit of expectancy for revival. Revival is not confined to structured and predictable church services but breaks free from religious constraints. It may disrupt our schedules and challenge our comfort zones.
- Like the early believers in Acts, we should long for the manifestation of the Spirit's power, being open to His leading and willing to embrace the unpredictable. Revival sparks when we are ready to step out in faith, trusting God to demonstrate His resurrection power through us.

Conclusion

- Raising the dead stands as a powerful testimony to God's authority over life and death. It is not a mere theological concept, or an extraordinary event reserved for the past.
- Through the Scriptures and modern-day testimonies, we see that raising the dead is a divine reality that we, as believers, can actively participate in.
- As we align our hearts with God's will, pray with faith, and boldly exercise our authority, we can ignite the dynamite of resurrection power in our lives, churches, and communities.
- Let us embrace the call to raise the dead, expecting revival and witnessing the transformational power of the Gospel in action.

Reflection

A summary of what you learnt in this lesson:

_____
_____
_____
_____
_____
_____
_____
_____
_____
_____
_____
_____
_____
_____
_____
_____
_____
_____

Reflection

30

How does this challenge you personally?

_____
_____
_____
_____
_____
_____
_____
_____
_____
_____
_____
_____
_____
_____
_____
_____
_____

Reflection

What is God saying to you personally?

_____
_____
_____
_____
_____
_____
_____
_____
_____
_____
_____
_____
_____
_____
_____
_____
_____
_____
_____
_____

Reflection

Group discussion notes:

_____
_____
_____
_____
_____
_____
_____
_____
_____
_____
_____
_____
_____
_____
_____
_____
_____
_____
_____
_____

APPLICATION

- _____
  _____
  _____
- _____
  _____
  _____
- _____
  _____
  _____
- _____
  _____
  _____
- _____
  _____
  _____

APPLICATION

AT HOME

How will you apply this practically in your life? (your response to the last reflection question)

- _____
_____
_____

- _____
_____
_____
_____

- _____
_____
_____

- _____
_____
_____

- _____
_____
_____
_____

Lesson 4

"Dreams & Visions"

Introduction

In this lesson, we will explore the supernatural phenomenon of dreams and visions, particularly in the context of revival.

We will examine the biblical foundations, testimonies, and various types of dreams and their interpretations.

It is essential to understand how God speaks to us through dreams and visions, discern true from false dreams, and effectively interpret the messages received.

As we delve into this topic, we will discover how dreams and visions play a significant role in igniting the power of revival and witnessing the miraculous work of God.

Lesson Outline

1. *The Prophetic Promise of Dreams and Visions*
- When God pours out His Spirit, one of the supernatural phenomena we can expect are dreams and visions.
- The Prophet Joel foretold this when he prophesied an end-time outpouring of the Holy Spirit. In Joel 2:28-29 it says:
- "And it shall come to pass afterward that I will pour out My Spirit on all flesh; your sons and your daughters shall prophesy, your old men shall dream dreams, your young men shall see visions. And also on My menservants and on My maidservants I will pour out My Spirit in those days." (Joel 2:28-29)
- This incredible promise of God's Spirit being poured out upon all flesh was fulfilled shortly after the resurrection of Christ. In Acts 2, the disciples of Jesus were gathered together, abiding faithfully in prayer as they waited for the promised outpouring of the Holy Spirit. Then, with the sound of a rushing wind, the Holy Spirit fell upon them and filled them all (Acts 2:1-4).

2. *Dreams and Visions in the Bible*
- Throughout the Bible, we see examples of God speaking to His people through dreams and visions. In the Old Testament God used dreams and visions to communicate with key individuals at crucial times. Abraham, Joseph, Daniel, and many others received divine guidance through dreams and visions. In the New Testament, the fulfillment of Joel's prophecy in Acts 2 demonstrates the continued relevance of dreams and visions in the outpouring of the Holy Spirit.

3. *Testimonies of God's Guidance through Dreams and Visions*
- Personal testimonies of individuals who have experienced God's guidance through dreams and visions provide powerful evidence of God's ongoing supernatural communication. These testimonies serve as a reminder that dreams and visions are not limited to a select few, but are available to all believers who have received the Holy Spirit. By sharing these testimonies, we can encourage others to seek and expect God's guidance through dreams and visions.

Lesson Outline

4. *Types of Dreams and Their Significance*
- *Warning Dreams*

Warning dreams serve as God's intervention and guidance in specific situations. Just as God warned Abimelech in a dream about taking Sarah and warned Joseph about King Herod's plans in a dream, He continues to warn and protect His people through dreams. These dreams can address sinful situations, impending danger, or areas in our lives that require correction.

- *Directional Dreams*

Directional dreams provide wisdom and guidance in making decisions or navigating geographical locations. Joseph's dreams about going to Egypt and returning from Egypt illustrate how God uses directional dreams to guide His people. By paying attention to these dreams, believers can follow God's leading and walk in His divine purposes.

- *Prophetic and Futuristic Dreams*

Prophetic and futuristic dreams reveal insights about future events and God's plans. Just as Daniel received apocalyptic dreams and visions concerning the end times, God continues to unveil His purposes through prophetic dreams. Understanding and interpreting these dreams help believers align themselves with God's plans and prepare for the future.

- *Indirect Dreams*

Sometimes, God uses other people's dreams to convey messages or insights to individuals. In Judges 7:13-15, Gideon overheard a man recounting a dream and its interpretation, which ultimately guided Gideon in his decision-making process. This example highlights the significance of being open to receiving God's message through the dreams of others. It emphasises the importance of unity and fellowship within the body of Christ, as God can use different individuals to speak to us and provide guidance.

Lesson Outline

5. *Interpreting Dreams and Avoiding Deception*
- Interpreting dreams is a gift from God, as seen in the example of Joseph interpreting Pharaoh's dreams (Genesis 41:25). However, it is crucial to interpret dreams in alignment with the Word of God to avoid deception. False dreams and visions can lead people astray, as warned in Jeremiah 23:32 and Zechariah 10:2. Therefore, believers should diligently test and discern the source and message of their dreams, ensuring that they align with the teachings of Scripture.

Conclusion

- The study of dreams and visions reveals the supernatural communication of God with His people throughout history.
- The fulfilment of Joel's prophecy in Acts 2 confirms the continued relevance of dreams and visions in the outpouring of the Holy Spirit.
- By exploring different types of dreams and their interpretations, believers can discern God's guidance, receive direction, and participate in the unfolding of God's plans. However, it is essential to approach dreams with discernment, grounded in the Word of God, to avoid deception and ensure that the messages received align with biblical truth.
- As we embrace this gift of dreams and visions, we can expect God to use them powerfully in the context of revival, leadin to transformed lives and the advancement of His Kingdom.

Reflection

A summary of what you learnt in this lesson:

_____
_____
_____
_____
_____
_____
_____
_____
_____
_____
_____
_____
_____
_____
_____
_____
_____
_____
_____
_____
_____

Reflection

How does this challenge you personally?

_____
_____
_____
_____
_____
_____
_____
_____
_____
_____
_____
_____
_____
_____
_____
_____
_____

Reflection

What is God saying to you personally?

_____

Reflection

Group discussion notes:

_____
_____
_____
_____
_____
_____
_____
_____
_____
_____
_____
_____
_____
_____
_____
_____
_____
_____
_____

APPLICATION

- _____
_____
_____
- _____
_____
_____
- _____
_____
_____
- _____
_____
_____
- _____
_____
_____
_____

APPLICATION

AT HOME

How will you apply this practically in your life? (your response to the last reflection question)

- _____
  _____
  _____
- _____
  _____
  _____
- _____
  _____
  _____
- _____
  _____
  _____
- _____
  _____
  _____

Lesson 5

The Power of the Gospel

Introduction

The Gospel of Jesus Christ is the most important message we will ever hear. It holds the power to ignite revival and bring about transformation.

In this lesson we will delve into the profound impact of the Gospel, its ability to save, and the necessity of understanding both the bad news and the good news.

By exploring scriptural references, we will gain a deeper appreciation for the power of the Gospel and its role in our lives and the lives of others.

Lesson Outline

1. *The Power of the Gospel*
- The Gospel is not just a message; it is the power of God for salvation (Romans 1:16).
- When the Gospel is preached and received with faith, it ignites the dynamite power of God. It is through the Gospel that people are saved, transformed, and set free.
- We must recognise the surpassing power of the Gospel and its central role in our lives and ministries.

2. *The Bad News*
- Before someone can fully appreciate the good news of the Gospel, they must understand the bad news.
- All have sinned and fallen short of God's glory (Romans 3:23); the penalty for sin is death, both physical and spiritual.
- Without the Gospel people remain separated from God, under His wrath, and unaware of the danger they are in.
- It is essential to communicate the bad news to help individuals realise their need for salvation.

3. *The Need for Repentance*
- Repentance is a vital part of receiving the Gospel. It involves turning away from sin and turning toward God.
- We must explain to people that they need to repent, make a complete U-turn in their lives, and choose to follow Jesus.
- Repentance is a transformative process empowered by God's grace, leading to a new life in Christ.

Lesson Outline

4. The Good News
- The Gospel is the ultimate good news!
- Through faith in Jesus Christ, we become new creations (2 Corinthians 5:17).
- The power of the Gospel makes us spiritually alive, reconciles us with God, and grants us eternal life. We receive forgiveness, righteousness, and adoption into God's family.
- The Gospel offers hope, freedom, and a new identity in Christ.

5. Sharing the Gospel
- As believers, we are called to share the Gospel with others.
- We must convey the bad news of sin, the need for repentance, and the transformative power of the Gospel.
- By using key verses such as Romans 3:23, Romans 6:23, and John 3:16, we can effectively communicate the central message of the Gospel.
- It is crucial to present the Gospel in its entirety, highlighting both the bad news and the good news.

6. The Role of Conviction
- The Holy Spirit convicts the world of sin, righteousness, and judgment (John 16:8).
- As we share the Gospel, it is essential to allow the Holy Spirit to work in the hearts of the listeners, bringing conviction and awareness of their need for salvation.
- The truth of the Gospel, when communicated in love and boldness, has the power to pierce through defenses and bring about genuine repentance.

Conclusion

- The Gospel is not just words on a page, it is the power of God unto salvation. It carries the potential to transform lives, reconcile us with God, and bring about revival.
- By understanding the bad news of sin, repenting, and embracing the good news of Jesus Christ, we experience the fullness of salvation and become partakers of His divine nature.
- As revival school students, we are called to boldly proclaim the Gospel, knowing that it holds the power to change lives and ignite revival.
- Let us embrace the dynamite power of the Gospel and be faithful messengers of this life-transforming message.

Reflection

A summary of what you learnt in this lesson:

_____
_____
_____
_____
_____
_____
_____
_____
_____
_____
_____
_____
_____
_____
_____
_____
_____
_____

Reflection

How does this challenge you personally?

Reflection

What is God saying to you personally?

_____
_____
_____
_____
_____
_____
_____
_____
_____
_____
_____
_____
_____
_____
_____
_____
_____
_____

Reflection

Group discussion notes:

_____
_____
_____
_____
_____
_____
_____
_____
_____
_____
_____
_____
_____
_____
_____
_____
_____
_____
_____
_____

APPLICATION

- _____
_____
_____
- _____
_____
_____
- _____
_____
_____
- _____
_____
_____
- _____
_____
_____

APPLICATION

AT HOME

How will you apply this practically in your life? (your response to the last reflection question)

- _____
  _____
- _____
  _____
  _____
- _____
  _____
  _____
- _____
  _____
  _____
- _____
  _____
  _____
  _____

Lesson 6

Discipled In Healing

Introduction

Divine health and healing is important in the Christian life (Mark 16:15). In this lesson we talk about personal experience and passion for divine healing.

Lesson Outline

1. Faith
- Understanding the role of faith in accessing divine healing (Mark 16:15; James 5:15).
- The power of faith in releasing healing to others (Mark 16:18)
- Key scripture: Romans 10:17 - "So then faith comes by hearing, and hearing by the word of God".

2. It's God's Will to Heal
- Clear biblical evidence of God's will to heal (Isaiah 53:5; Psalm 103:2-3).
- Scriptures affirming God's heart and will for divine healing (Exodus 15:26).
- The unchanging nature of God and His will for healing (Hebrews 13:8).
- Personal testimony and experiences of healing.

3. The Atonement
- Jesus' sacrifice for healing in the atonement (Isaiah 53:5).
- Understanding the Hebrew word "Rapha" and its usage for physical healing (Exodus 15:26).
- New Testament confirmation of physical healing in the atonement (Matthew 8:16-17).

4. Our Authority
- Recognising the authority given to believers in Christ (2 Corinthians 5:20).
- Understanding the power and authority to release healing (Acts 3:1-8).
- Personal testimonies of exercising authority and witnessing miracles.
- Embracing the role of ambassadors for Christ and acting on His behalf (Proverbs 18:21).

Conclusion

- Encouragement to pursue healing and step into the authority given (Mark 16:15-18).
- Examples from the Bible (Peter, disciples) demonstrating the power of authority in healing.
- Calling to follow Jesus' commission to lay hands on the sick and see them recover (Mark 16:18).

Reflection

A summary of what you learnt in this lesson:

_____
_____
_____
_____
_____
_____
_____
_____
_____
_____
_____
_____
_____
_____
_____
_____
_____
_____
_____
_____

Reflection

How does this challenge you personally?

_____
_____
_____
_____
_____
_____
_____
_____
_____
_____
_____
_____
_____
_____
_____
_____
_____
_____
_____
_____

Reflection

What is God saying to you personally?

Reflection

Group discussion notes:

_____
_____
_____
_____
_____
_____
_____
_____
_____
_____
_____
_____
_____
_____
_____
_____
_____
_____
_____
_____

APPLICATION

-
-
-
-
-

APPLICATION

AT HOME

How will you apply this practically in your life? (your response to the last reflection question)

- _____
- _____
- _____
- _____
- _____

Lesson 7

It's For All Believers

Introduction

In this lesson we will explore the importance of understanding that all believers can operate in the supernatural.

As we gain a deeper understanding of the supernatural, we will address common misconceptions and doubts.

Lesson Outline

1. Igniting the Dynamite
- New Christians often demonstrate child-like faith and quicker understanding.
- Unraveling doubt and false doctrines hindering faith (2 Timothy 3:5).
- The power of personal testimonies and mentorship (Proverbs 28:1).

2. Everyone Can Operate in the Supernatural
- Jesus' commission to all believers to heal the sick and cast out demons (Luke 10:1-12).
- The Great Commission includes discipleship in the supernatural (Matthew 28:20).
- Challenging the idea that supernatural power is limited to a select few.

3. Already Qualified
- Emphasising the importance of pursuing leadership roles and Bible College (1 Timothy 3:1).
- Recognising that external recognition does not determine one's ability to operate in signs and wonders.
- The moment of being born-again and filled with the Spirit as the qualification to ignite the dynamite.

4. Not A Spectator
- Equating the role of a Christian to a football game.
- Importance of coaching and equipping by Church leaders.
- Acknowledging that what happens "on the field" is what truly matters (2 Corinthians 5:18).
- Encouraging every Christian to actively participate and engage in the game.

Conclusion

- Understanding the presence of the Holy Spirit within every believer.
- Examples of ordinary believers operating in signs and wonders (Acts 6:8).
- Encouragement to ignite the dynamite in all areas of life.

Reflection

A summary of what you learnt in this lesson:

_____
_____
_____
_____
_____
_____
_____
_____
_____
_____
_____
_____
_____
_____
_____
_____
_____
_____
_____
_____

Reflection

How does this challenge you personally?

_____
_____
_____
_____
_____
_____
_____
_____
_____
_____
_____
_____
_____
_____
_____
_____
_____
_____

Reflection

What is God saying to you personally?

_____
_____
_____
_____
_____
_____
_____
_____
_____
_____
_____
_____
_____
_____
_____
_____
_____
_____
_____
_____

Reflection

Group discussion notes:

_____
_____
_____
_____
_____
_____
_____
_____
_____
_____
_____
_____
_____
_____
_____
_____
_____
_____
_____
_____

APPLICATION

- _____
  _____
  _____
- _____
  _____
  _____
- _____
  _____
  _____
- _____
  _____
  _____
- _____
  _____
  _____
  _____

APPLICATION

AT HOME

How will you apply this practically in your life? (your response to the last reflection question)

- _____
- _____
- _____
- _____
- _____

Lesson 8

Cessationism

Introduction

We will explore Daniel Hagen's personal experience of encountering cessationism in a Baptist Church and discover the differences in beliefs among Christians. We will discuss desiring to see the supernatural power of God at work.

Lesson Outline

1. *Understanding Cessationism*
- Definition of Cessationism and its beliefs
- The cessationist view on the gifts of the Spirit and miracles (1 Corinthians 12, 13, 14)
- Examining the purpose of the gifts and their alleged cessation (Hebrews 1:1-2)

2. *The Need for Supernatural Power*
- Embracing the call to operate in signs, wonders, and miracles (Mark 16:17-18)
- Recognising Jesus' promise of greater works for believers (John 14:12)
- Understanding the continuing relevance of the five-fold ministry (Ephesians 4:11)

3. *Correct Interpretation of Scripture (Hermeneutics)*
- Importance of studying the whole Bible and its context (2 Peter 1:19)
- Examining examples of the Holy Spirit leading and speaking today (Acts 16:6-7)
- Challenging flawed interpretations that support Cessationism

4. *The Role of the Holy Spirit Today*
- Acknowledging the ongoing work of the Holy Spirit (John 15:26)
- Understanding the conviction and guidance provided by the Spirit (John 16:8)
- Examining the supernatural empowerment for ministry (Mark 13:9-11)

Conclusion

- Reflecting on personal experiences of God's supernatural power
- Encouragement to study and interpret scripture accurately.
- Embracing the Holy Spirit's leading and operating in signs and wonders.

Reflection

A summary of what you learnt in this lesson:

_____
_____
_____
_____
_____
_____
_____
_____
_____
_____
_____
_____
_____
_____
_____
_____
_____

Reflection

How does this challenge you personally?

_____
_____
_____
_____
_____
_____
_____
_____
_____
_____
_____
_____
_____
_____
_____
_____
_____
_____

Reflection

What is God saying to you personally?

_____
_____
_____
_____
_____
_____
_____
_____
_____
_____
_____
_____
_____
_____
_____
_____
_____
_____

Reflection

Group discussion notes:

_____
_____
_____
_____
_____
_____
_____
_____
_____
_____
_____
_____
_____
_____
_____
_____
_____
_____

APPLICATION

- _____
_____
_____
- _____
_____
_____
- _____
_____
_____
- _____
_____
_____
- _____
_____
_____

APPLICATION

AT HOME

How will you apply this practically in your life? (your response to the last reflection question)

- _____
  _____
  _____
- _____
  _____
  _____
- _____
  _____
  _____
- _____
  _____
  _____
- _____
  _____
  _____

Lesson 9

Ignite the Dynamite! The Empowerment of the Holy Spirit

Introduction

Key Scripture
"But you shall receive power when the Holy Spirit has come upon you; and you shall be witnesses to Me in Jerusalem, and in all Judea and Samaria, and to the end of the earth."

We're living a supernatural life empowered by the Holy Spirit.
This power we receive is the miracle-working power of God.
The baptism of the Holy Spirit is essential for our discipleship and calling.

Lesson Outline

1. Examples of Empowerment

Apollos

- Apollos only understood the baptism of John until Priscilla and Aquila explained the more accurate way.
- The baptism of the Holy Spirit is the more accurate way.
- Apollos became a major leader in the early Church after receiving the baptism of the Holy Spirit.

John G. Lake

- John G. Lake's ministry exploded after receiving the baptism of the Holy Spirit.
- His healing ministry brought about significant impact and transformation.

2. Seeking the Baptism of the Holy Spirit

- Personal testimony of seeking and receiving the baptism of the Holy Spirit.
- The experience of being filled with the Holy Spirit and speaking in tongues.
- The ongoing manifestations of God's power and presence in daily life.

3. The Five Baptisms of the Spirit in Acts

- The Upper Room (Acts 2:1-4): The outpouring on the Day of Pentecost.
- Paul the Apostle in Damascus (Acts 9:17-18): Paul's encounter with the Holy Spirit.
- Philip and the City of Samaria (Acts 8:14-17): The manifestation of the Holy Spirit's power.
- The Household of Cornelius (Acts 10:44-46): The pouring out of the Holy Spirit on the Gentiles.
- Paul at Ephesus (Acts 19:6-7): The Holy Spirit's manifestation through speaking in tongues and prophesying.

4. Continual Filling of the Holy Spirit

- The believers in Acts 4 were filled with the Holy Spirit again.
- Hungering and thirsting for the continual outpouring of the Holy Spirit.
- Igniting the dynamite within through faith and the Word of God.

Conclusion

- Faith ignites the dynamite of the Holy Spirit within us.
- The study guide and the book aim to ignite the dynamite in every sphere of society.
- The Holy Spirit empowers us to be witnesses and impact the world for Christ.

Reflection

A summary of what you learnt in this lesson:

_____
_____
_____
_____
_____
_____
_____
_____
_____
_____
_____
_____
_____
_____
_____
_____
_____
_____

Reflection

How does this challenge you personally?

Reflection

What is God saying to you personally?

_____
_____
_____
_____
_____
_____
_____
_____
_____
_____
_____
_____
_____
_____
_____
_____
_____
_____
_____

Reflection

Group discussion notes:

APPLICATION

- _____
  _____
  _____
- _____
  _____
  _____
- _____
  _____
  _____
- _____
  _____
  _____
- _____
  _____
  _____

APPLICATION

AT HOME

How will you apply this practically in your life? (your response to the last reflection question)

- _____
  _____
  _____
- _____
  _____
  _____
- _____
  _____
  _____
- _____
  _____
  _____
- _____
  _____
  _____

Study Notes

1. Take notes on key concepts and scriptures.
2. Reflect on personal experiences and testimonies of healing and operating in the supernatural.
3. Engage in group discussions or study sessions to share insights and learn from others.
4. Memorize key scriptures related to healing and faith.
5. Meditate on the examples of healing in the Bible and consider their implications for your own life and ministry.
6. Seek practical opportunities to apply the principles learned, such as praying for the sick and expecting healing.
7. Continuously seek a deeper understanding of divine healing through further study and prayer.
8. Challenge any doubts or misconceptions about your ability to walk in signs and wonders.
9. Meditate on scriptures that affirm the presence of the Holy Spirit and the power within you.
10. Engage in mentorship or discipleship relationships to strengthen your faith and understanding.
11. Seek opportunities to step out in faith and practice operating in the supernatural, both inside and outside of Church gatherings.
12. Stay connected to a community of believers who support and encourage the pursuit of the supernatural.
13. Engage in discussions with believers from different denominations to gain different perspectives.
14. Seek out testimonies and teachings from individuals who operate in signs, wonders, and miracles.
15. Continuously study and deepen your understanding of God's Word and His promises regarding the supernatural.
16. Seek guidance from the Holy Spirit in understanding and applying scripture.
17. Deep dive into scriptures that speak about the gifts of the Spirit and their purpose.
18. Study passages related to the ministry of Jesus and the early disciples in the New Testament
19. Develop a solid foundation in hermeneutics to interpret scripture accurately.
20. Stay rooted in prayer and cultivate a personal relationship with the Holy Spirit.

Additional Resources

a) Explore the teachings and experiences of renowned healing ministers, such as Jack Coe, Katheryn Kuhlman, Smith Wigglesworth, John G. Lake, and A.A. Allan.

b) Read books or listen to sermons on divine healing and the authority of believers in Christ.

c) Engage with revival schools, conferences.

d) Read books on the topic of the gifts of the Spirit and the role of the Holy Spirit in the Church today.

e) Listen to sermons and teachings from renowned pastors and teachers who emphasise the supernatural.

f) Attend conferences or events that focus on revival and the operation of the gifts of the Spirit.

g) Engage in practical exercises and activations to develop and grow in the supernatural gifts.

h) Seek out mentorship or discipleship relationships with experienced and mature believers in operating in signs and wonders.

i) Seek teachings and testimonies from experienced believers who operate in signs and wonders.

j) Read books or listen to sermons on the topic of supernatural ministry and the authority of all believers.

k) Attend conferences or events focused on revival, where you can learn from seasoned ministers and receive impartation.

l) Engage in prayer and fasting to strengthen your spiritual connection and sensitivity to the Holy Spirit's leading.

m) Practice sharing your faith and praying for others regularly, both within your local Church and in everyday life.

www.ingramcontent.com/pod-product-compliance
Lightning Source LLC
Chambersburg PA
CBHW061138010526

44107CB00069B/2981